5

k brown

26

BODY WIDTH

2

20

CHARACTER WIDTH

CAP HEIGHT

11

27 os over

33

15

14

24

10

ASCENDER HEIGHT

X-HEIGHT

19 y dog.

6

13

30

22

25

23

/ 4. ARM / 5. ASCENDER / 6. AXIS / 7. BEAK / 8. BILATERAL SERIF / 9. BOWL
(CLOSED) / 12. CROSSBAR / 13. CROTCH / 14. DESCENDER / 15. EAR / 16. EYE
LINE / 20. LEG / 21. LIGATURE / 22. LINK (NECK) / 23. LOOP / 24. OVERHANG
NE / 28. SPUR / 29. STEM / 30. TAIL / 31. TITTLE / 32. TERMINAL / 33. VERTEX

THIS JOURNAL BELONGS TO

All rights reserved.
Published in the United States by
Clarkson Potter/Publishers,
an imprint of the Crown Publishing Group,
a division of Penguin Random House LLC,
New York.
crownpublishing.com
clarksonpotter.com

CLARKSON POTTER is a trademark and
POTTER with colophon is a registered
trademark of Penguin Random House LLC.

Library of Congress Cataloging-in-
Publication Data is available on request

ISBN 978-0-451-49572-3

Printed in China

Book and cover design
by Nina Simoneaux

10 9 8 7 6 5 4 3 2 1

First Edition

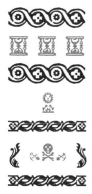

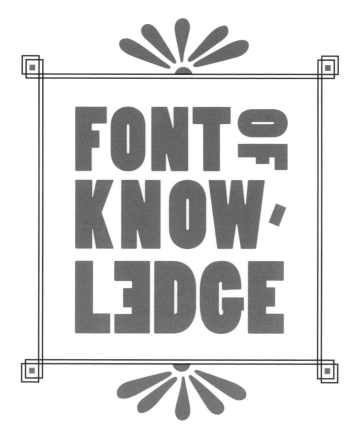

FONT OF KNOW-LEDGE

•••• A Journal of Facts and Fonts ••••

CLARKSON POTTER/PUBLISHERS

NEW YORK

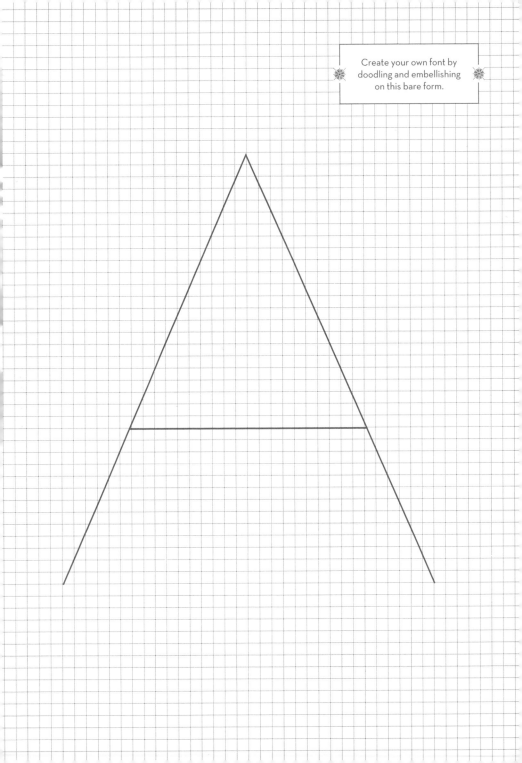

Create your own font by doodling and embellishing on this bare form.

6

8

10

12

14

16

18

20

22

24

26

PTS.   A   B   C   D   E   F   G   H   I   J   K   L   M

ALBERTUS

† ✳ † ✳ †
✕ † ✳ † ✕
† ✳ † ✳ †
✕ † ✳ † ✕
† ✳ † ✳ †
✕ † ✳ † ✕
† ✳ † ✳ †
✕ † ✳ † ✕
† ✳ † ✳ †
✕ † ✳ † ✕
† ✳ † ✳ †

Named for Albertus Magnus, the thirteenth-century German philosopher and theologian, Albertus is the typeface used on British coinage.

† ✳ † ✳ †
✕ † ✳ † ✕
† ✳ † ✳ †
✕ † ✳ † ✕
† ✳ † ✳ †

N O P Q R S T U V W X Y Z

8

10

12

14

16

18

20

22

24

26

PTS.   A   B   C   D   E   F   G   H   I   J   K   L   M

Designed in 1936 by Hans Bohn for the Ludwig & Mayer type foundry, Allegro became commercially popular in the mid-twentieth century because of its versatility: It is at once roman and italic, fat-face and stencil, modern and script.

N O P Q R S T U V W X Y Z

8

10

12

14

16

18

20

22

24

26

A   B   C   D   E   F   G   H   I   J   K   L   M

ARCHER

This neo-grotesque slab serif can be found in

- *Martha Stewart Living* magazine

- the Wells Fargo branding

- the Wes Anderson film *The Grand Budapest Hotel*

N O P Q R S T U V W X Y Z

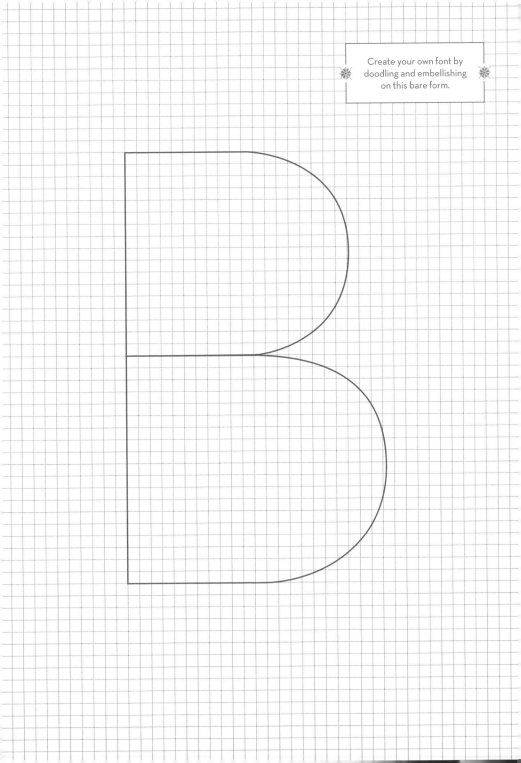

Create your own font by
doodling and embellishing
on this bare form.

6

8

10

12

14

16

18

20

22

24

26

PTS.　A　B　C　D　E　F　G　H　I　J　K　L　M

Designed by
John Baskerville
in 1757, Basker-
ville is classified
as a transitional
typeface; the
increased contrast
between thick
and thin strokes,
sharper more-
tapered serifs,
and vertical axis
create consistency
in size and form.

N O P Q R S T U V W X Y Z

6

8

10

12

14

16

18

20

22

24

26

PTS.   A   B   C   D   E   F   G   H   I   J   K   L   M

TRUE or FALSE

This variant of
URW Blippo Black
can be found in
the Postman Pat
logo and around
Disney's Polyne-
sian Village Resort.

True

ANSWER

N O P Q R S T U V W X Y Z

6

8

10

12

14

16

18

20

22

24

26

PTS.   A   B   C   D   E   F   G   H   I   J   K   L   M

Based on a design cut by Francesco Griffo for printer Aldus Manutius, Bembo is named for Manutius's first publication, the 1496 book by poet and cleric Pietro Bembo.

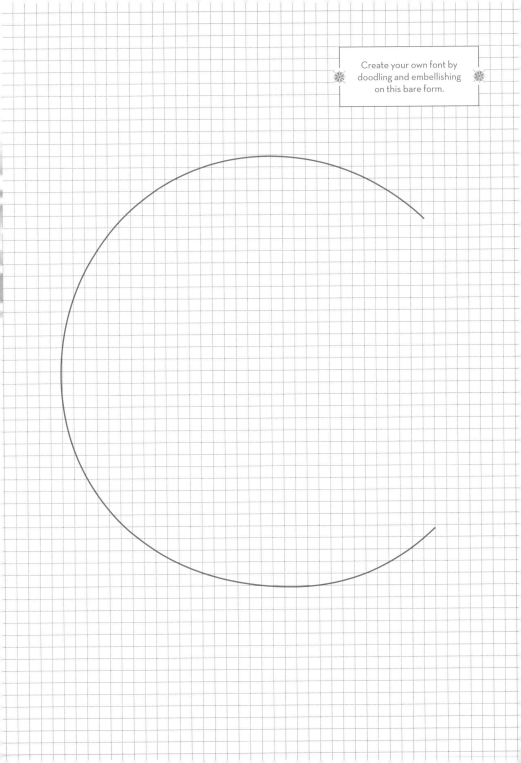

Create your own font by
doodling and embellishing
on this bare form.

6

8

10

12

14

16

18

20

22

24

26

PTS.　　A　B　C　D　E　F　G　H　I　J　K　L　M

First published in 1845, the original Clarendon had no uppercase letters and is considered the first registered typeface.

N O P Q R S T U V W X Y Z

6

8

10

12

14

16

18

20

22

24

26

PTS.   A   B   C   D   E   F   G   H   I   J   K   L   M

FAMOUS FOR
ITS NO-FRILLS
CAPITALS,
COPPERPLATE
GOTHIC WAS
THE TYPEFACE
USED ON THE
LOGO OF *WHO
WANTS TO BE
A MILLIONAIRE,*
AND IT WAS THE
UNIVERSAL
PICTURES LOGO
FROM 1997
TO 2012.

N   O   P   Q   R   S   T   U   V   W   X   Y   Z

6

8

10

12

14

16

18

20

22

24

26

PTS.   A   B   C   D   E   F   G   H   I   J   K   L   M

COURIER NEW

Courier New
was actually
created by
digitizing the
script on an
IBM typeball;
the outlines
are thinner
than those of
the original
font because
the type-
creator's ball
was designed
deliberately
thinner than
the intended
character
stroke width
to avoid
bleeding
when the ink
soaked into
the paper.

N   O   P   Q   R   S   T   U   V   W   X   Y   Z

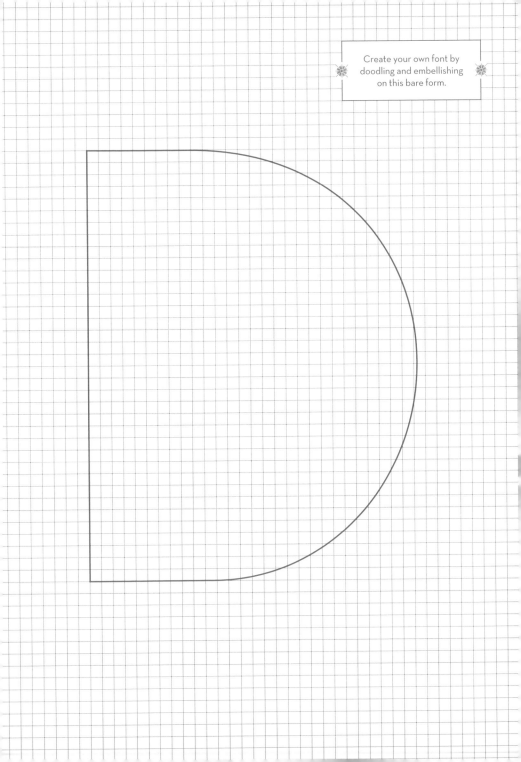

Create your own font by doodling and embellishing on this bare form.

6

8

10

12

14

16

18

20

22

24

26

PTS.   A   B   C   D   E   F   G   H   I   J   K   L   M

Didot was
developed in
Paris between
1784 and 1811,
and was used
to print *La
Henriade* by
Voltaire.

N O P Q R S T U V W X Y Z

6

8

10

12

14

16

18

20

22

24

26

PTS.   A   B   C   D   E   F   G   H   I   J   K   L   M

DIN 1451

»«»«»«»«»«

↑ ↓ ↑ ↓

≤≥ ≤≥
↓ ⥮ ↓ ⥮

≤≥ ≤≥
⥮ ↓ ⥮ ↓

≤≥ ≤≥
↓ ⥮ ↓ ⥮

≤≥ ≤≥
⥮ ↓ ⥮ ↓

≤≥ ≤≥
↓ ⥮ ↓ ⥮

DIN 1451 is
a sans-serif
typeface widely
used for traffic,
administrative,
and technical
applications.
DIN stands for
Deutsches
Institut für Nor-
mung or German
Institute for
Standardization.

↓ ↑ ↓ ↑

≤≥ ≤≥
⥮ ↓ ⥮ ↓

≤≥ ≤≥
↓ ⥮ ↓ ⥮

≤≥ ≤≥
↓ ⥮ ↓ ⥮

≤≥ ≤≥
↓ ⥮ ↓ ⥮

N O P Q R S T U V W X Y Z   »«»«»«»«»«

6

8

10

12

14

16

18

20

22

24

26

PTS.　　A　　B　　C　　D　　E　　F　　G　　H　　I　　J　　K　　L　　M

*!!!
$
#!&@
@ * *
#?!
!! * $$$ *
@ XXX $
* * $
!!! @

Designed to
emulate brush
script, Dom
Casual has
been used often
in television
credits, as on
Bewitched and
Barney Miller,
as well as
Warner Bros.
cartoons appear-
ing between
1960–64.

#!&@

N O P Q R S T U V W X Y Z

6

8

10

12

14

16

18

20

22

24

26

PTS.   A   B   C   D   E   F   G   H   I   J   K   L   M

Edward Benguiat designed Edwardian Script by hand in 1994 in a nod to calligraphy, drawing and redrawing each letter until the connective elements of the letters were perfected in order to create the look of true handwriting.

N O P Q R S T U V W X Y Z

EGYPTIENNE

Egyptienne is
a slab serif:
the serifs are
unbracketed
and similar
in weight to
the horizontal
strokes of the
letters.

N   O   P   Q   R   S   T   U   V   W   X   Y   Z

6

8

10

12

14

16

18

20

22

24

26

PTS. A B C D E F G H I J K L M

EUROSTILE

€Ł »
« 73
æ æ
✳✳ Œ
ᴲ ✳✳
¤ ● ¤ ●
● ¤ ● ¤

&U
★ ★ ★ ★

Created originally
for one of the
best-known Italian
foundries, Nebiolo
of Turin, Eurostile
was designed as
the next incarna-
tion of the popular
Microgramma,
created to include
a lowercase
alphabet that
was missing in
its predecessor.

★ ★ ★ ★
å å å å
》《 》《 》《

Ø

N O P Q R S T U V W X Y Z

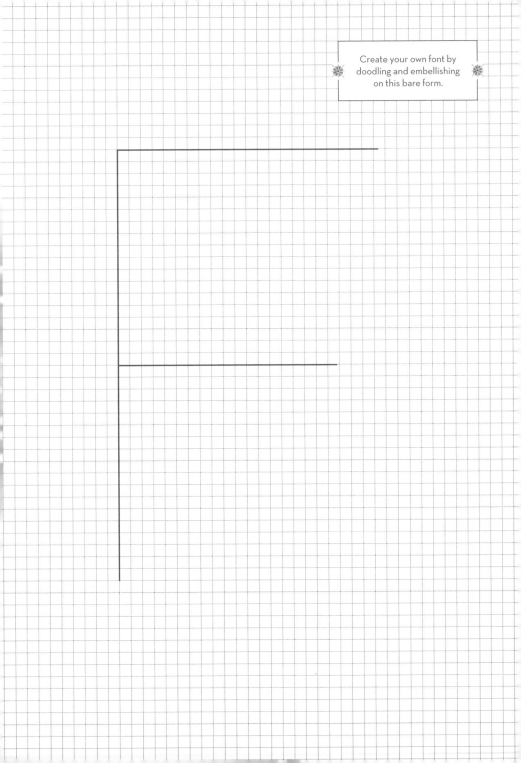

Create your own font by
doodling and embellishing
on this bare form.

6

8

10

12

14

16

18

20

22

24

26

PTS.   𝔄 𝔅 ℭ 𝔇 𝔈 𝔉 𝔊 ℌ ℑ 𝔍 𝔎 𝔏 𝔐

Fraktur is a blackletter typeface that became widely known during the Protestant Reformation in Germany.

N O P Q R S T U V W X Y Z

6

8

10

12

14

16

18

20

22

24

26

PTS. A   B   C   D   E   F   G   H   I   J   K   L   M

FRANKLIN GOTHIC

Franklin Gothic can be distinguished from other sans serifs by

- double-story

a AND g

- the tail of the

- the ear of the

N   O   P   Q   R   S   T   U   V   W   X   Y   Z

6

8

10

12

14

16

18

20

22

24

26

PTS.   A   B   C   D   E   F   G   H   I   J   K   L   M

FUTURA

Originally created by Paul Renner in 1927, the near-perfect circles, triangles, and squares of Futura remain commercially popular to this day, toted by Ikea, Crayola, and Party City.

N   O   P   Q   R   S   T   U   V   W   X   Y   Z

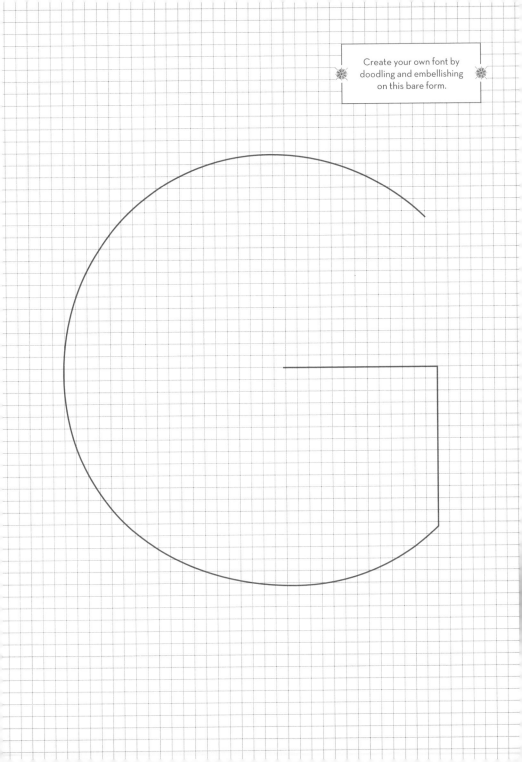

Create your own font by
doodling and embellishing
on this bare form.

6

8

10

12

14

16

18

20

22

24

26

PTS.   A   B   C   D   E   F   G   H   I   J   K   L   M

GEORGIA

Designed for
clarity on a
computer
monitor even
at small sizes,
Georgia
features

- a large
  x-height

- tall lowercase
  letters

- thicker
  strokes than
  usual on a
  higher
  resolution
  typeface

N O P Q R S T U V W X Y Z

6

8

10

12

14

16

18

20

22

24

26

PTS. | A B C D E F G H I J K L M

GOTHAM

||||||||||||||||||||||||

Originally com-
missioned for
GQ magazine,
the Gotham
typeface can
be seen on the
Freedom Tower
and was used
in the Obama
presidential
campaign in
2008 and 2012.

N   O   P   Q   R   S   T   U   V   W   X   Y   Z ||||||||||||||||||||||||||||

6

8

10

12

14

16

18

20

22

24

26

PTS.   A   B   C   D   E   F   G   H   I   J   K   L   M

Based on the Garamond typeface that was used in a book printed by the Parisian Jean Poupy in 1592, Granjon was used in *Mastering the Art of French Cooking,* vols. I and II, by Julia Child, Simone Beck, and Louisette Bertholle.

N O P Q R S T U V W X Y Z

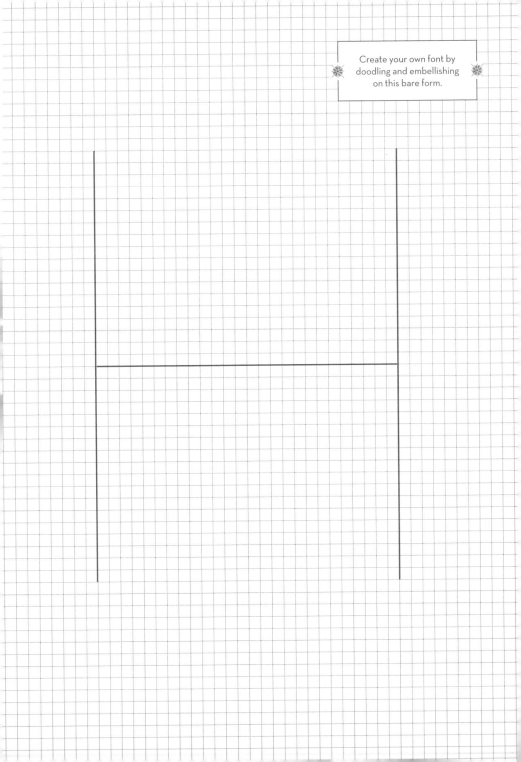

Create your own font by
doodling and embellishing
on this bare form.

8

10

12

14

16

18

20

22

24

26

A   B   C   D   E   F   G   H   I   J   K   L   M

HELVETICA

✚

Helvetica, developed in 1957 by Swiss typeface designer Max Miedinger, is unique because all its strokes termi- nate on exactly horizontal or vertical lines.

✚   ✚

✚

✚   ✚

✚

✚   ✚

✚

✚   ✚

✚

N   O   P   Q   R   S   T   U   V   W   X   Y   Z ✚   ✚

6

8

10

12

14

16

18

20

22

24

26

PTS.　A　ß　C　D　E　F　G　H　I　J　K　L　M

Designed in 1993, Hoffmann was created based on letters traced and cut out by lettering artist Lothar Hoffmann.

N O P Q R S T U V W X Y Z

Designed in 1936
by Hans Bohn
for the Ludwig
& Mayer type
foundry, this font
became commer-
cially popular in
the mid-twentieth
century because of
its versatility: It is
at once straight
and italic, fat-
face and stencil,
modern and script.

N O P Q R S T U V W X Y Z

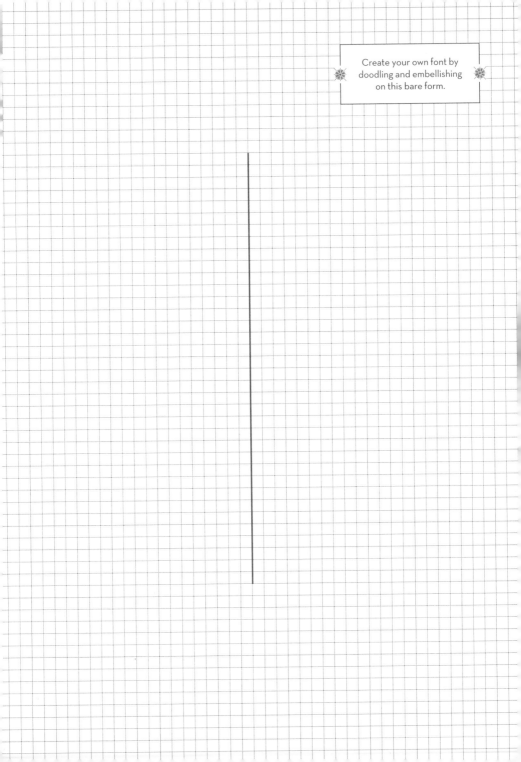

Create your own font by
doodling and embellishing
on this bare form.

6

8

10

12

14

16

18

20

22

24

26

PTS. A B C D E F G H I J K L M

IMPACT

,, ,, ,, ,, ,,
×
,, ,, ,, ,, ,,
×
,, ,, ,, ,, ,,
×
,, ,, ,, ,, ,,
×
,, ,, ,, ,, ,,

Designed by
Geoffrey Lee in
1965, Impact is a
realist sans-serif
typeface whose
main impact is
being one of the
core fonts distrib-
uted with the
Microsoft
Windows web
package.

,, ,, ,, ,, ,,
×
,, ,, ,, ,, ,,
×
,, ,, ,, ,, ,,
×
,, ,, ,, ,, ,,
×
,, ,, ,, ,, ,,
×

N   O   P   Q   R   S   T   U   V   W   X   Y   Z   ,, ,, ,, ,, ,,

6

8

10

12

14

16

18

20

22

24

26

PTS.   A   B   C   D   E   F   G   H   I   J   K   L   M

Originally created by Neville Brody for *The Face* magazine in 1984, Industria's geometric lines can be found in the logos of the NBA's Oklahoma City Thunder and the MLS's New York Red Bulls.

6

8

10

12

14

16

18

20

22

24

26

PTS.   A   B   C   D   E   F   G   H   I   J   K   L   M

Ionic is one of
the typefaces
designed by
Chauncey H.
Griffith that
belong to his
"Legibility
Group," which
contains fonts
especially
suited to news-
print including
Corona, Excel-
sior, Opticon,
Paragon, and
Textype.

N O P Q R S T U V W X Y Z

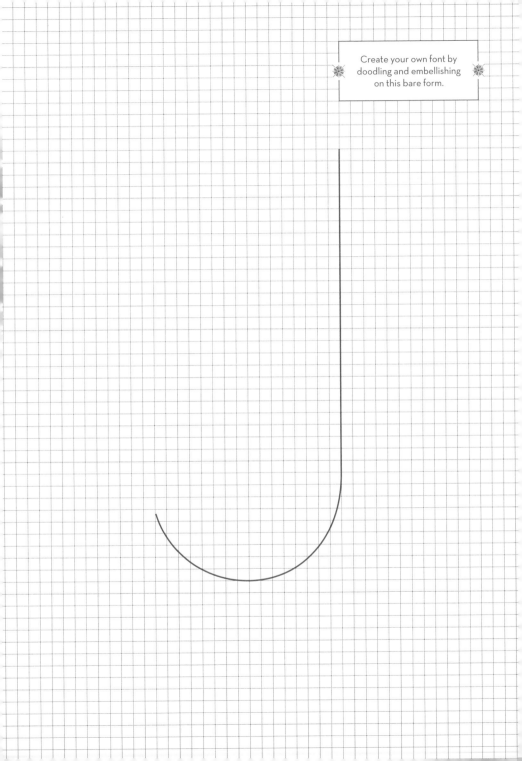

Create your own font by doodling and embellishing on this bare form.

6

8

10

12

14

16

18

20

22

24

26

PTS.   A   B   C   D   E   F   G   H   I   J   K   L   M

JANSON

Wrongly named for Anton Janson, a seventeenth-century Dutch punchcutter (creator of the steel letters from which copper type is then made), Janson was actually designed by Hungarian punchcutter Miklos Kis while he was in Amsterdam in 1685.

N O P Q R S T U V W X Y Z

JOANNA

Named for one of
the daughters of its
designer Eric Gill,
Joanna was chosen
to set *An Essay on
Typography* so that
the book would be
"face free from all
fancy business."

N O P Q R S T U V W X Y Z

6

8

10

12

14

16

18

20

22

24

26

PTS.   A B C D E F G H I J K L M

A GEOMETRIC
SANS SERIF
DESIGNED BY
LUIS SIQUOT,
JUANITA
REFLECTS
DESIGNS THAT
ORIGINATED IN
THE 1930S AND
40S AND WERE
STILL POPULAR
DURING
SIQUOT'S
CHILDHOOD IN
THE 1950S.

N O P Q R S T U V W X Y Z

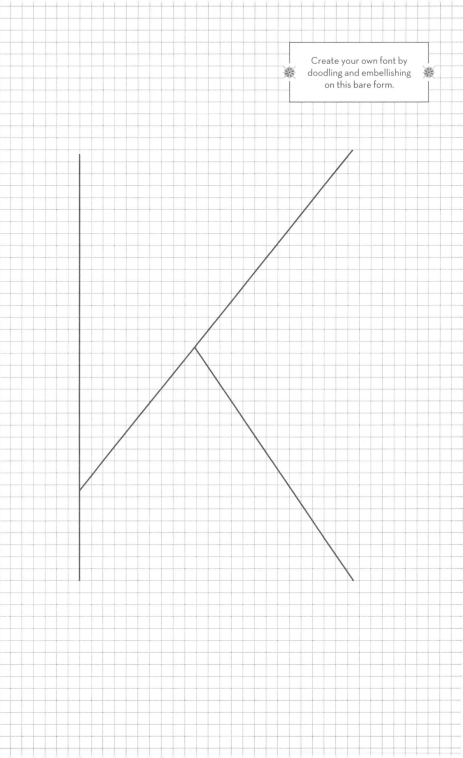

6

8

10

12

14

16

18

20

22

24

26

PTS.   A   B   C   D   E   F   G   H   I   J   K   L   M

Named after cable cars of the 1920s, Kabel is a geometric sans serif often looked at as the twin of the 1922 font Koch Antiqua — both share qualities such as character shape and proportion, and most notably their peculiar g.

6

8

10

12

14

16

18

20

22

24

26

PTS.   A   B   C   D   E   F   G   H   I   J   K   L   M

A brush script
typeface created
by Max R.
Kaufmann in
1936, Kaufmann
features

- a monotone stroke
  weight
- freely drawn
  uppercase letters
- lowercase letters
  of regular height
  and width

N O P 2 R S T U V W X Y 3

6

8

10

12

14

16

18

20

22

24

26

PTS.　　A　　B　　C　　D　　E　　F　　G　　H　　I　　J　　K　　L　　M

With thirty-two
versions in its family,
Knockout is beloved
for its functionality
and known as the
"American Sans Serif."

Create your own font by
doodling and embellishing
on this bare form.

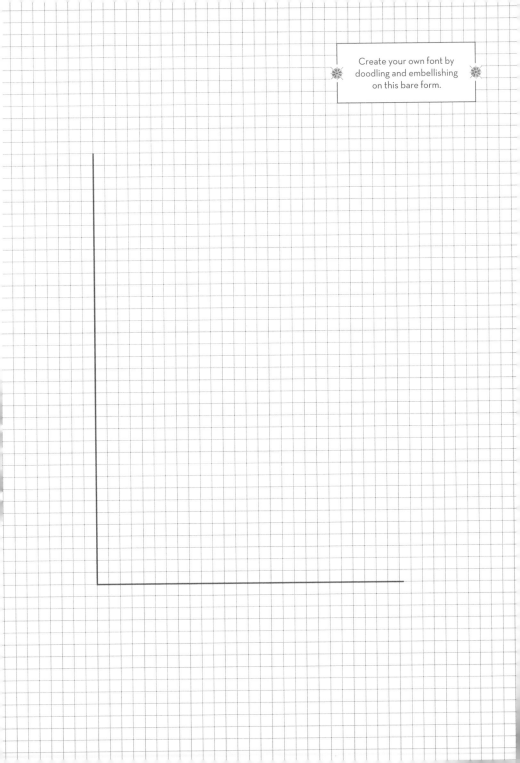

8

10

12

14

16

18

20

22

24

26

PTS.   A   B   C   D   E   F   G   H   I   J   K   L   M

In a nod to painter, print-maker, draughts-man, and illus-trator Henri de Toulouse-Lautrec, *Le Petit Trottin* is a stylized semi-serif created by Luiz Da Lombra in 2001.

N   O   P   Q   R   S   T   U   V   W   X   Y   Z

6

8

10

12

14

16

18

20

22

24

26

PTS.   A   B   C   D   E   F   G   H   I   J   K   L   M

Created in 1974,
Lubalin Graph
is based on
Herb Lubalin's
earlier Avant
Garde Gothic,
with the added
feature of slab
serifs and an
x-height that is
extremely high
compared to its
descender and
ascender.

N O P Q R S T U V W X Y Z

6

8

10

12

14

16

18

20

22

24

26

PTS.   A   B   C   D   E   F   G   H   I   J   K   L   M

Created by Warren
Chappell in 1938,
Lydian's stressed
letter designs
and rounded
capitals suggest a
calligraphic style,
despite the fact
that it is considered
a sans-serif font.

N   O   P   Q   R   S   T   U   V   W   X   Y   Z

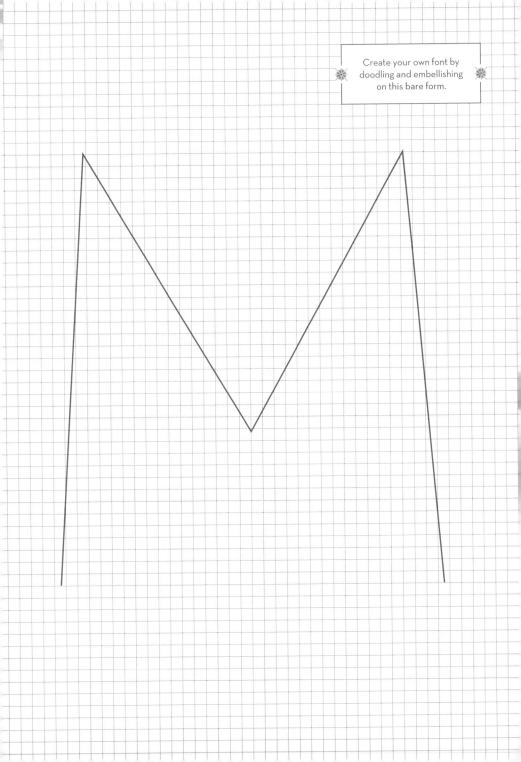

Create your own font by
doodling and embellishing
on this bare form.

PTS.   A   B   C   D   E   F   G   H   I   J   K   L   M

Designed by Rudolph Wolf in 1929, Memphis is the first revival of the popular Egyptian serif from the 1800s in Germany, including geometric letter shapes and stems and serifs that have the same weight values.

6

8

10

12

14

16

18

20

22

24

26

PTS.　　A　　B　　C　　D　　E　　F　　G　　H　　I　　J　　K　　L　　M

MERCURY

A favorite of newspapers such as the *New York Times*, Mercury was designed to perform on a wide range of formats, from screens to printed pages. It underwent nine years of development for readability before being released in 1996 by Hoefler & Frere-Jones.

6

8

10

12

14

16

18

20

22

24

26

PTS. A   B   C   D   E   F   G   H   I   J   K   L   M

↦◦↤◇↦◦↤

~❋~

↦ « ∫s » ↤

~☼~

↦◦↤◇↦◦↤

A variant of Baskerville, Mrs Eaves is a transition serif designed by Zuzana Licko in 1996 to be used in display contexts such as headings and book blurbs through low x-height and a range of unusually combined ligatures.

↦◦↤◇↦◦↤

~✢~

I ·∞· † ·∞· I

~❀~

↦ « ffi » ↤

~❋~

N O P Q R S T U V W X Y Z ↦◦↤◇↦◦↤

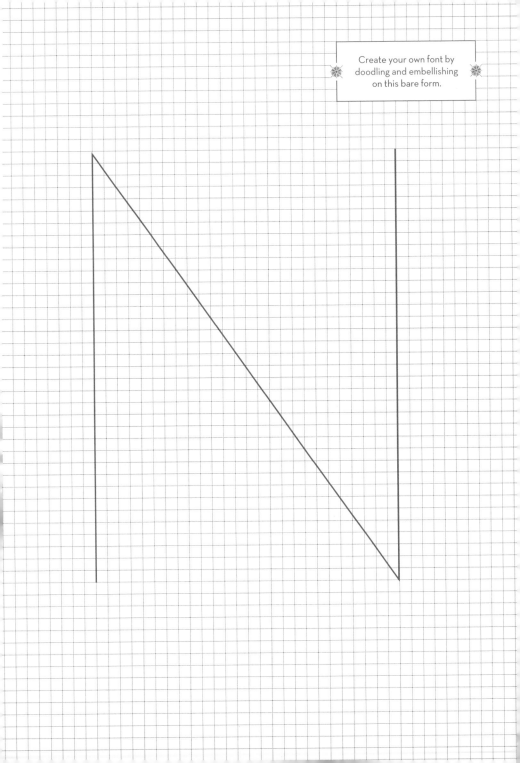

Create your own font by doodling and embellishing on this bare form.

A realist sans
serif, News
Gothic was
designed by
Morris Fuller
Benton and
released in
1908, fol-
lowing the
grotesque
model with
a two-story
lowercase
a and *g*.

N O P Q R S T U V W X Y Z

6

8

10

12

14

16

18

20

22

24

26

PTS. A B C D E F G H I J K L M

Designed
by Robin
Nicholas in
1980, Nimrod
is a favorite
of newspapers
and book
publishing,
and is the face
of the UK's
Guardian and
*The Concise
English
Dictionary.*

N O P Q R S T U V W X Y Z

6

8

10

12

14

16

18

20

22

24

26

PTS.   A   B   C   D   E   F   G   H   I   J   K   L   M

Created in
2000 by James
Montalbano,
Nora is a decora-
tive hand-lettered
font.

N O P Q R S T U V W X Y Z

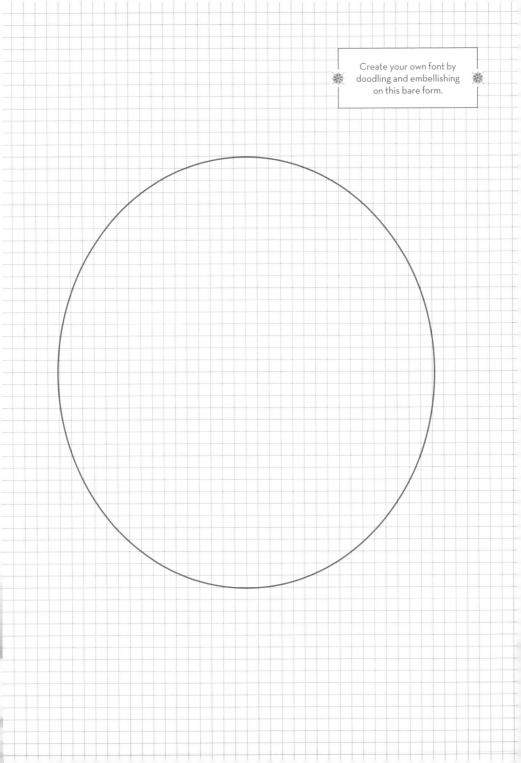

Create your own font by
doodling and embellishing
on this bare form.

6

8

10

12

14

16

18

20

22

24

26

PTS.   𝔄   𝔅   ℭ   𝔇   𝔈   𝔉   𝔊   ℌ   ℑ   𝔍   𝔎   𝔏   𝔐

Ideal for certificates, diplomas, or any other documents requiring an air of stateliness and authority, Old English was designed by the Monotype Corporation to have regal initial capitals and a legible lowercase, with roots in calligraphy.

N O P Q R S T U V W X Y Z

6

8

10

12

14

16

18

20

22

24

26

PTS.   A   B   C   D   E   F   G   H   I   J   K   L   M

ONYX

Onyx is one of many variants on the nineteenth-century fat-faced theme, with condensed and highly contrasted elements aimed at style, not readability.

N O P Q R S T U V W X Y Z

PTS.   A   B   C   D   E   F   G   H   I   J   K   L   M

A humanist
font released by
Hermann Zapf
between 1952
and 1955,
Optima's capitals
are derived from
the classic Roman
monumental cap-
ital mode, with
strokes variable
in width.

N O P Q R S T U V W X Y Z

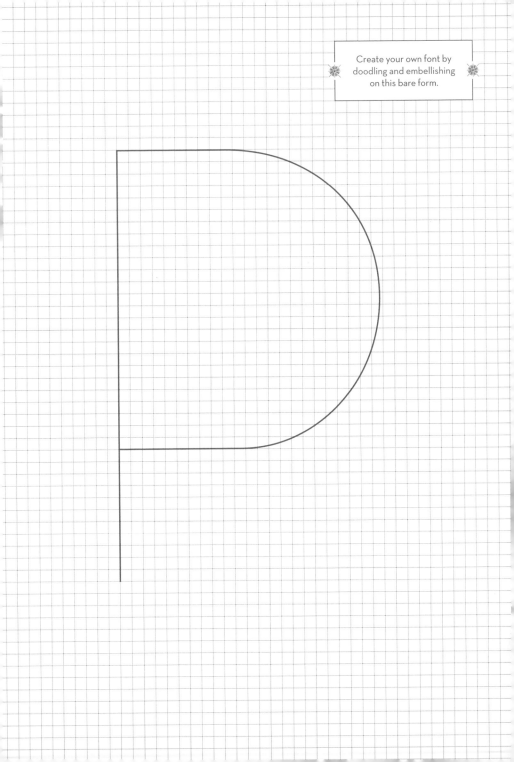

Create your own font by
doodling and embellishing
on this bare form.

6

8

10

12

14

16

18

20

22

24

26

PTS.   A   B   C   D   E   F   G   H   I   J   K   L   M

Designed by
Morris Fuller
Benton in 1928,
Parisian features
the application of
pure geometric
form to a sans serif
and is a touchstone
of its swinging era.

N O P Q R S T U V W X Y Z

8

10

12

14

16

18

20

22

24

26

PTS.   A   B   C   D   E   F   G   H   I   J   K   L   M

CREATED by A. M. CASSANDRE iN 1937, PEIGNOT ExpERIENCEd A popuLARiTy suRGE iN THE 1970s wHEN pEoplE sAw iTs muLTi-CASE LowERCASE (A mix of CApiTAL ANd LowER-CASE LETTERs) iN THEiR LiviNG ROOMs oN *THE MARY TyLER MOORE SHOw* CREdiTs.

N   O   P   Q   R   S   T   U   V   W   X   Y   Z

6

8

10

12

14

16

18

20

22

24

26

PTS.   A   B   C   D   E   F   G   H   I   J   K   L   M

Created by Robert
Harling in 1938, the
letters of Playbill are
derived from so-called
woodtypes, well known
through their popular
use in wanted posters
and Westerns.

N O P Q R S T U V W X Y Z

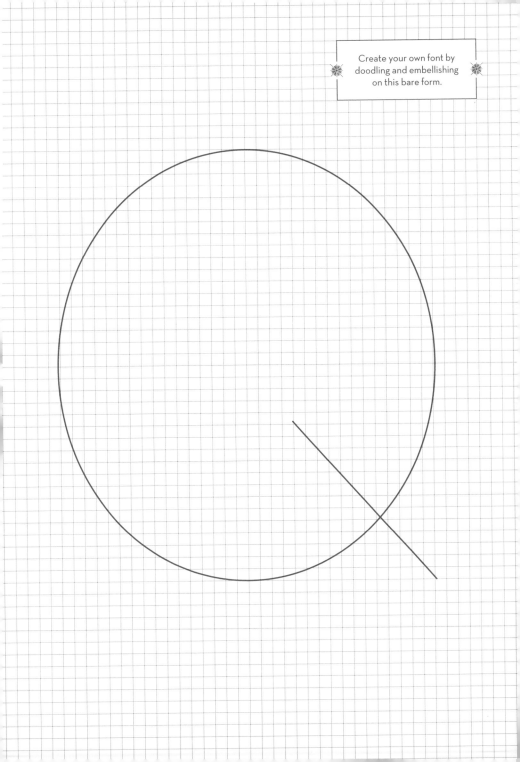

6

8

10

12

14

16

18

20

22

24

26

PTS.   A   B   C   D   E   F   G   H   I   J   K   L   M

Originally designed
in the Netherlands,
Quadraat com-
bines Renaissance
elegance with con-
temporary ideas on
construction and
shaping.

N O P Q R S T U V W X Y Z

6

8

10

12

14

16

18

20

22

24

26

PTS.   A B C D E F G H I J K L M

Based on the font shown in the title sequence for the 2008 James Bond film *Quantum of Solace.* Quantum comes in five varieties and was created by Ænigma.

N O P Q R S T U V W X Y Z

A B C D E F G H I J K L M

Created by
Ray Baker in
1977, Quorum
is comprised
of character
shapes that
are essentially
oval, with the
basic character
structure of a
sans serif but
with sharp
flared stroke
endings that
look almost
like serifs.

N O P Q R S T U V W X Y Z

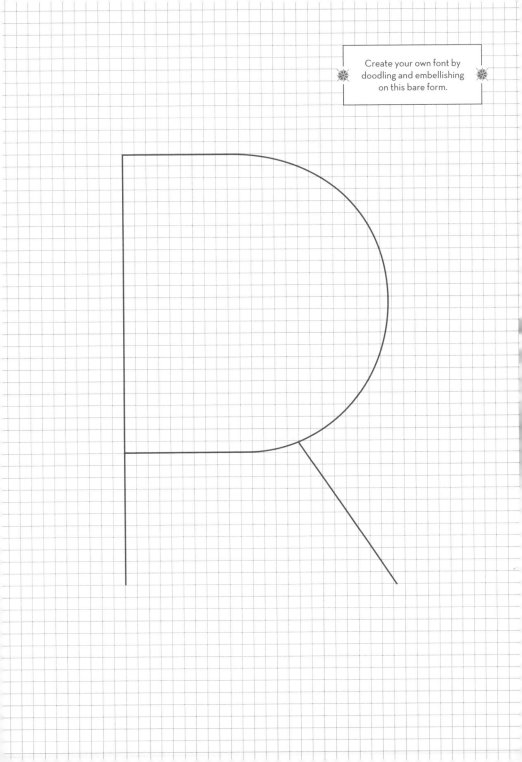

Create your own font by
doodling and embellishing
on this bare form.

6

8

10

12

14

16

18

20

22

24

26

PTS.　A　B　C　D　E　F　G　H　I　J　K　L　M

- - - - - - -

A slab serif
designed by
Monotype in
1934, Rockwell
is known for the
distinctive serif
at the apex of
its uppercase
A and its incon-
gruous two-
story lowercase
a. It is the font
used by the
CW Television
Network and
the Charlotte
Hornets.

- - - - - - -

°**ØOo a oOØ**°

- - - - - - -

- - - - - - -

°**ØOo a oOØ**°

- - - - - - -

°**ØOo a oOØ**°

- - - - - - -

N   O   P   Q   R   S   T   U   V   W   X   Y   Z   - - - - - - -

6

8

10

12

14

16

18

20

22

24

26

PTS.   A   B   C   D   E   F   G   H   I   J   K   L   M

ADOBE'S
ROSEWOOD,
RELEASED
IN 1994, IS A
BI-COLOR SLAB
SERIF MODELED
AFTER CLAREN-
DON ORNAMENT-
ED, WHICH WAS
FIRST SHOWN
BY WILLIAM
H. PAGE IN HIS
1874 *SPECIMENS
OF CHROMATIC
WOOD TYPE,
BORDERS, ETC.*

N O P Q R S T U V W X Y Z

6

8

10

12

14

16

18

20

22

24

26

PTS.   A   B   C   D   E   F   G   H   I   J   K   L   M

Developed in 1988
by Otl Aicher, Rotis
is an exploration in
maximum legibility
that is widely used
across industries,
including

- the back cover
  of Bjork's album,
  Homogenic

- PNC Financial
  Services

- Scandinavian
  Airlines

N O P Q R S T U V W X Y Z

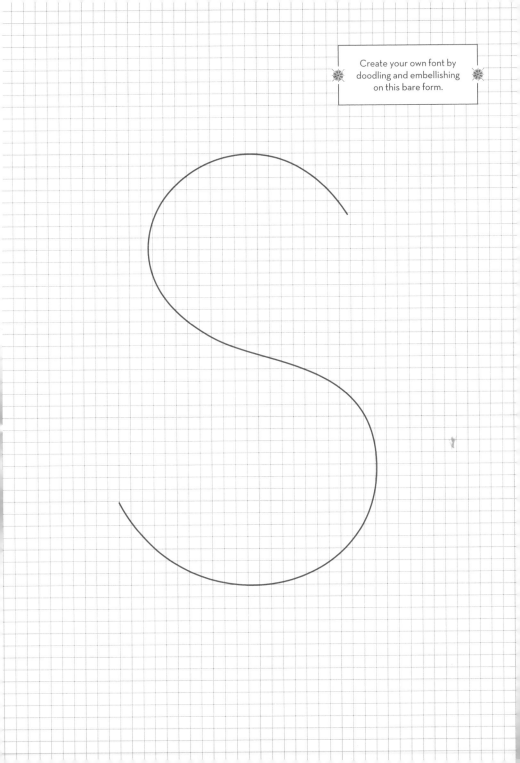

8

10

12

14

16

18

20

22

24

26

PTS. | A B C D E F G H I J K L M

A slab serif
typeface
designed by
Adrian Frutiger
in 1964, Serifa
was prominently
featured in

- the Montgom-
  ery Ward logo

- Ross Perot's
  1992 presiden-
  tial campaign

- CBS news
  programs in
  the 1980s

6

8

10

12

14

16

18

20

22

24

26

PTS.   A   B   C   D   E   F   G   H   I   J   K   L   M

Hugely popular in the 1970s, Souvenir became pinned as a *Saturday Night Fever* typeface and faced a huge backlash in the 1980s, similar to the one to be faced by Comic Sans a decade later.

N O P Q R S T U V W X Y Z

6

8

10

12

14

16

18

20

22

24

26

PTS.　A　B　C　D　E　F　G　H　I　J　K　L　M

STENCIL

TWO STENCIL **TYPEFACES WERE RELEASED WITHIN A MONTH OF EACH OTHER IN 1937— ONE BY R. HUNTER MIDDLETON AND ONE BY GERRY POWELL, WHICH IS STILL POPULAR TODAY. BOTH FONTS HAVE**

- **ONLY CAPITAL LETTERS**
- **ROUNDED EDGES**
- **THICK MAIN STROKES**

N O P Q R S T U V W X Y Z

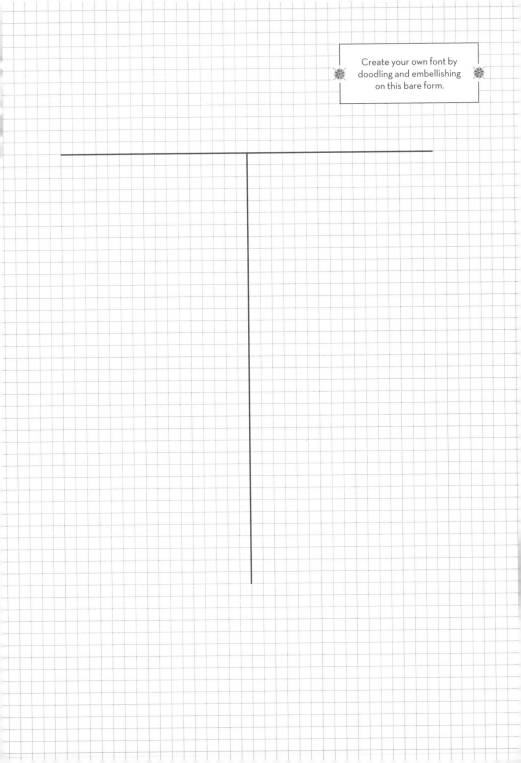

Create your own font by doodling and embellishing on this bare form.

6

8

10

12

14

16

18

20

22

24

26

PTS.   A   B   C   D   E   F   G   H   I   J   K   L   M

TIMES NEW ROMAN

Originally commissioned by the UK newspaper, *The Times,* in 1931, Times is an old-style serif with short ascenders and descenders and a high x-height that saves space and increases clarity overall while showcasing a condensed aesthetic.

§

N O P Q R S T U V W X Y Z

6

8

10

12

14

16

18

20

22

24

26

PTS.   A   B   C   D   E   F   G   H   I   J   K   L   M

Created by
Alessandro Butti
in 2001, Torino
was originally
designed as a
metal typeface in
1908 by the font
foundry Nebiolo
in Turin (from
which its name
was derived).

N   O   P   Q   R   S   T   U   V   W   X   Y   Z

6

8

10

12

14

16

18

20

22

24

26

A   B   C   D   E   F   G   H   I   J   K   L   M

TRADE
GOTHIC

Designed by
Jackson Burke
in 1948, Trade
Gothic is used
by Amnesty Inter-
national and
Vice magazine.

N O P Q R S T U V W X Y Z

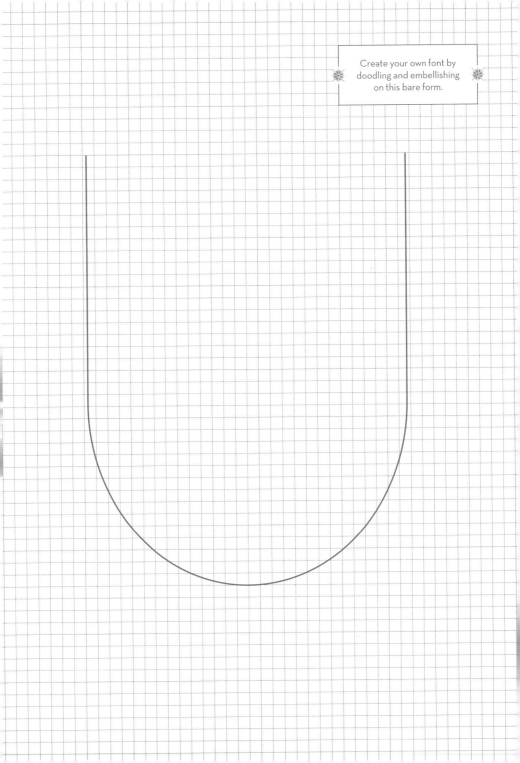

Create your own font by doodling and embellishing on this bare form.

6

8

10

12

14

16

18

20

22

24

26

PTS. A   B   C   D   E   F   G   H   I   J   K   L   M

DESIGNED
IN 1935 BY
R. HUNTER
MIDDLETON,
UMBRA IS A
SANS-SERIF
DISPLAY TYPE-
FACE THAT IS
AN ADAPTA-
TION OF THE
UPPERCASE
SET OF THE
EARLIER TYPE-
FACE TEMPO
LIGHT; ITS
NAME REFERS
TO THE SHAD-
OW SPACES
THAT CREATE
THE ACTUAL
LETTERS.

N O P Q R S T U V W X Y Z

10

12

14

16

18

20

22

24

26

A   B   C   D   E   F   G   H   I   J   K   L   M

Created by
Adrian Frutiger
in 1954, Univers
is a sans-serif
typeface mod-
eled after the
1898 typeface
Akzidenz-
Grotesk.

N   O   P   Q   R   S   T   U   V   W   X   Y   Z

6

8

10

12

14

16

18

20

22

24

26

PTS.   A   B   C   D   E   F   G   H   I   J   K   L   M

Designed by
Leslie Usher-
wood in 1984,
Usherwood is
an informal and
personable type-
face with hints
of Goudy, Baur,
and Augusta.

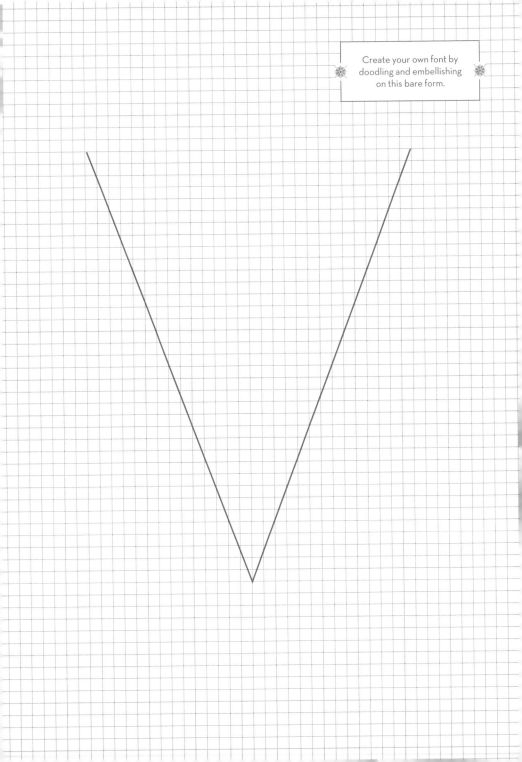

Create your own font by doodling and embellishing on this bare form.

6

8

10

12

14

16

18

20

22

24

26

PTS.   A   B   C   D   E   F   G   H   I   J   K   L   M

Designed by
Gerry Barney,
VAG Rounded
is a geometric
sans serif with
rounded termini
in every stroke
created originally
for the Volks-
wagen AG motor
manufacturer in
1964.

N O P Q R S T U V W X Y Z

8

10

12

14

16

18

20

22

24

26

Created by Hoefler
& Frere-Jones in
2006, Verlag was
originally designed
as a variation on
the Guggenheim's
iconic Art Deco
lettering.

N O P Q R S T U V W X Y Z

6

8

10

12

14

16

18

20

22

24

26

PTS.

A B C D E F G H I J K L M

Created by
Adrian Frutiger
in 1984, Versailles
was influenced
by the French
Latine metal
lettering—a style
characterized
by very sharp
triangular serifs—
on a memorial
for Charles
Garnier, the
designer of the
Paris Opera
building.

N O P Q R S T U V W X Y Z

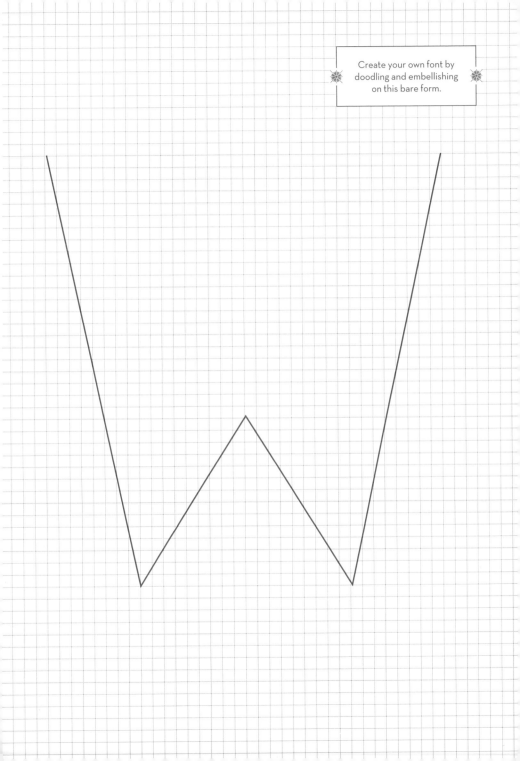

6

8

10

12

14

16

18

20

22

24

26

PTS. | A B C D E F G H I J K L M

WEIDEMANN

✝ ± ✝ ± ✝ ± ✝

✝ ± ✝ ± ✝ ± ✝

✝ ± ✝ ± ✝ ± ✝

✝ ± ✝ ± ✝ ± ✝

✝ ± ✝ ± ✝ ± ✝

✝ ± ✝ ± ✝ ± ✝

Designed by Kurt
Weidemann in
1983, this font
was originally
named Biblica and
was commissioned
for the collabora-
tive publication of
the Bible by the
German Catholic
and Protestant
Churches.

✝ ± ✝ ± ✝ ± ✝

✝ ± ✝ ± ✝ ± ✝

✝ ± ✝ ± ✝ ± ✝

N O P Q R S T U V W X Y Z ✝ ± ✝ ± ✝ ± ✝

6

8

10

12

14

16

18

20

22

24

26

A glyphic font,
Weiss was created
in 1926 by leg-
endary self-taught
calligrapher, Emil
Rudolf Weiss.

N O P Q R S T U V W X Y Z

6

8

10

12

14

16

18

20

22

24

26

PTS.   A   B   C   D   E   F   G   H   I   J   K   L   M

WINDSOR

Designed by
Eleisha Pechey,
Windsor was
intended for dis-
play and heading
use; its capital
M and *W* are
widely splayed,
and its capital *P*
and *R* have very
large bowls, all
of which make
a statement on
the page.

N O P Q R S T U V W X Y Z

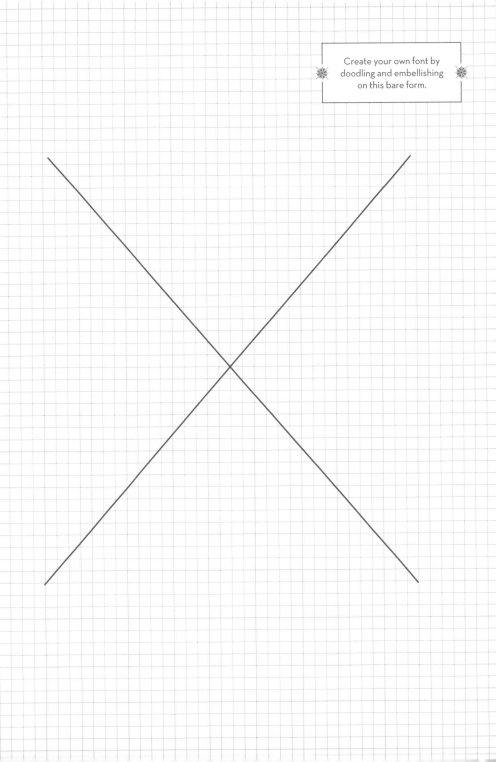

Create your own font by
doodling and embellishing
on this bare form.

6

8

10

12

14

16

18

20

22

24

26

PTS.   A   B   C   D   E   F   G   H   I   J   K   L   M

Xander has free
proportioned
headset characters,
with high contrast
and reverse
camber faces in
connection with
the main points
of the stroke.

6

8

10

12

14

16

18

20

22

24

26

PTS.   A   B   C   D   E   F   G   H   I   J   K   L   M

Originally created in 1924 by Benjamin Krebs, Xylo saw an update in 1995 after it was discovered in a London printer's reference book.

N O P Q R S T U V W X Y Z

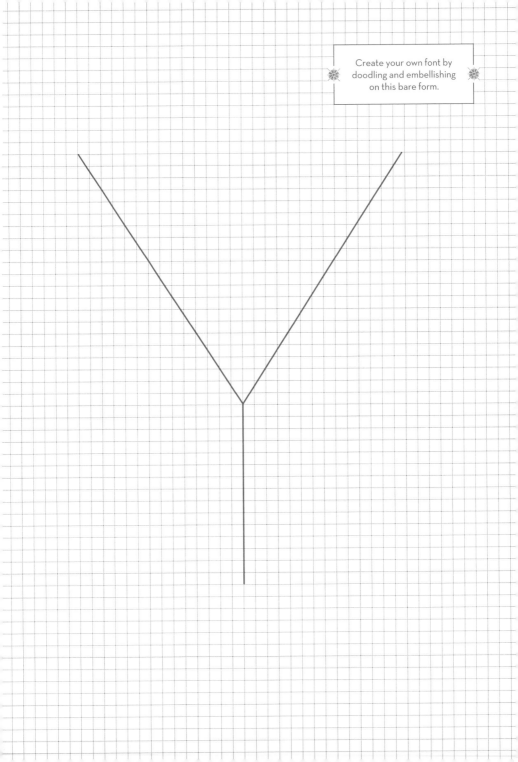

Create your own font by
doodling and embellishing
on this bare form.

6

8

10

12

14

16

18

20

22

24

26

PTS.   A   B   C   D   E   F   G   H   I   J   K   L   M

YEARLING

Created by
Chank Diesel in
2000, Yearling
was originally
conceived to
work well in
print through
fax machines
and computer
monitors; it was
built on a simple
grid system with
an emphasis on
horizontal and
vertical strokes
and a limited use
of diagonals.

N O P Q R S T U V W X Y Z

Originally
published by
Stephenson
Blake in
1952 as a
copperplate script
for the banking
and insur-
ance industries,
Youthline was
re-released in
1955 as a
headline and
invitation font.

N O P Q R S T U V W X Y Z

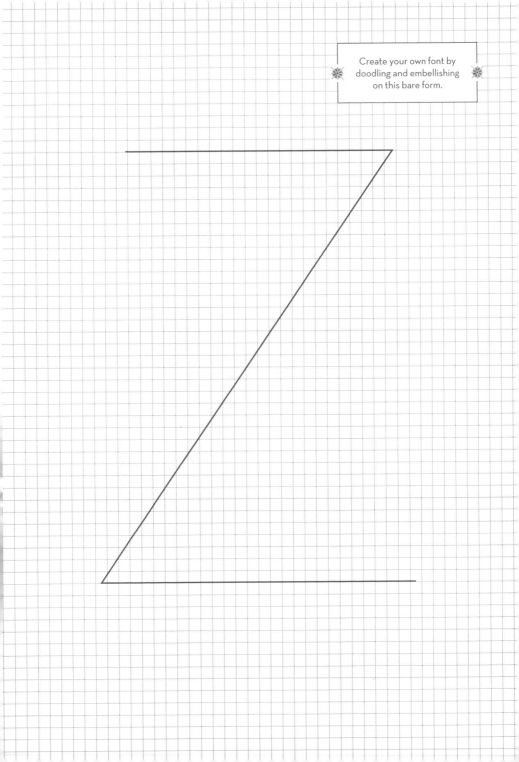

Create your own font by doodling and embellishing on this bare form.

6

8

10

12

14

16

18

20

22

24

26

PTS.   A   B   C   D   E   F   G   H   I   J   K   L   M

Designed in 1976 by Hermann Zapf, Zapf Book combines characteristics of Walbaum, Mecior, and Bodini.

N O P Q R S T U V W X Y Z

6

8

10

12

14

16

18

20

22

24

26

PTS.	A B C D E F G H I J K L M

ZAPF CHANCERY

§

§

§

§

§

§

§

§

§

§

§

§

§

§

§

§

§

§

§

Designed by
Hermann Zapf in
1979, Zapf Chancery
is one of the three
main typefaces
shipped with
computers running
MAC OS as one of
the core PostScript
fonts.

§

§

§

N O P Q R S T U V W X Y Z §

6

8

10

12

14

16

18

20

22

24

26

PTS. A   B   C   D   E   F   G   H   I   J   K   L   M

ZURICH

Created by
Adrian Frutiger
in 2000, Zurich
is oft looked
upon as an
updated version
of Univers.

N   O   P   Q   R   S   T   U   V   W   X   Y   Z

Sources

myfonts.com
ehow.com
ilovetypography.com
linotype.com
typography.com
fonts.com
typedia.com
fontfont.com
fontshop.com
fontsplace.com
luc.devroye.org
wikipedia.org